The DRAWING BOOK FOR KIDS: DOGS

Step by Step with Space to Practice

Published by Turner Publishing Company

The Drawing Book for Kids: Dogs — Step by Step with Space to Practice

Woo! Jr. Kids Activities Founder: Wendy Piersall

Art Director/Instructions Writted and Illustrated by: Lilia Garvin

Cover Illustration: Michael Koch | Sleeping Troll Studios www.sleepingtroll.com

Interior Illustration: Avinash Saini

9781684420629 Paperback

9781684420773 Hardcover

How to use This Book!

All you need is a pencil and eraser!

Follow each drawing diagram step by step:

Tips:

Draw lightly at first, because you might need to erase some lines as you work.

Add details according to the diagrams, but don't worry about being perfect! Artists frequently make mistakes - they just find ways to make their mistakes look interesting. You can erase mistakes, or use use them as a new decoration.

Don't worry if your drawings don't turn out quite the way you want them to. Just keep practicing! Sometimes drawing the same thing just a few times will help.

You can draw a new animal every day or several each day. For an extra challenge, use your creativity to combine multiple animals into an entire scene.

Want to add more Detail?

You can introduce shading techniques to make your drawings even more realistic and fun! Once you have finished your lines, consider shading in one of these ways:

Shading Technique: Hatching

In hatching, draw lots of lines that don't cross. You can press harder with your pencil to make darker lines, and space them closer together for a more full, consistent gradient (in art, a **gradient** is a transition from one color or shade to another.)

Anywhere you put marks on the paper it will look darker. For your lightest spots, don't put any marks.

Shading Technique: Cross-Hatching

Cross-hatching is very similar to hatching. The key difference is that you now also want to make marks coming from a second direction. Practice this technique with pencil or pen. They're both very good materials to cross-hatch with!

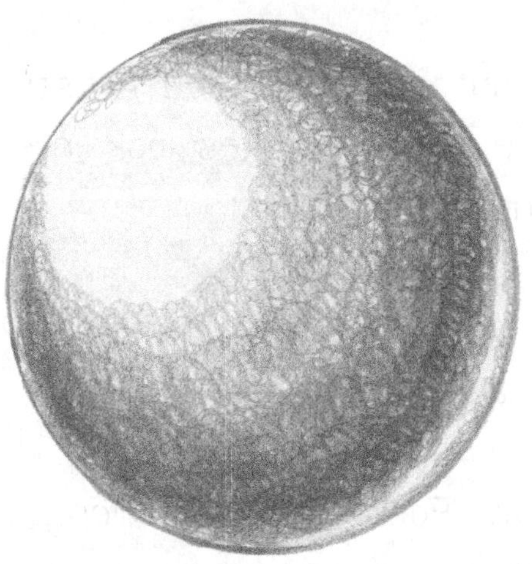

Shading Technique: Scumbling

Scumbling is a method where you shade with much more random marks than hatching, or cross-hatching. To scumble, use circular and squiggling marks. Don't worry what direction your pencil is moving in. Try to keep your wrist loose, and relax.

Remember to overlap, or layer, your marks, and put them closer together in your darkest areas.

Shading Technique: Stippling

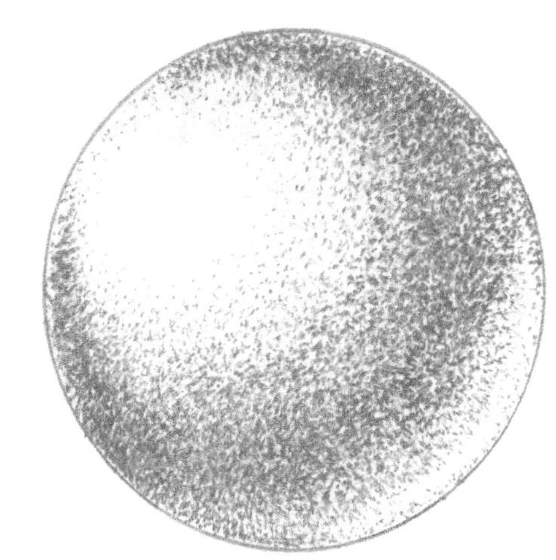

Stippling is also known as **pointillism**. To stipple, you shade with many, many small dots. This is a bit similar to how pixels are used to shade on a computer screen.

The closeness, or density, of your dots will determine your darkest points. Choose a starting point, and then carefully lift your pencil or pen up, and press down to make your dots. Try to avoid making any lines, or marks.

Shading Technique: Blending

With blending, the marks you make on the paper don't matter as much. You can start with hatched, cross-hatched, or scumbled marks. Try to make your shading smooth, and close together.

Next, rub the pencil marks together. You can use a facial tissue, napkin, or even your fingers. Afterward, make sure to clean your hands when you're done. It's messy!

Practicing Value

Example

In art, value means the degree of lightness or darkness of a color. Right now, since we're shading with pencil, that color is black, and the variation in value is called a **greyscale**. We're going to practice making them.

Use the scale to shade from light to dark. The paper can be your lightest shade. Press a bit harder for each new shade, until you get to the darkest.

You can practice here ...**and here!**

If you want to practice more, you can! First, draw a line of squares. Use a ruler to help you, or any hard surface. It's okay if the lines aren't perfect - then shade!

Step-By-Step Shading

Step 1: Complete your Linework

Find the animal you want to draw by skimming through the book. For this example, we're going to be shading the Akita found on page 14.

Follow the steps to draw your animal, and then make the lines dark by pressing hard with your pencil, or inking over your lines with a pen. If you decide to ink with a pen, wait for the ink to dry and erase the pencil marks underneath.

Step 2: Decide your method

Let's decide how to shade this good dog. Because our Akita is a furry dog, it looks like hatching would be good at replicating the texture of fur. We're going to hatch lightly with a pencil, to make the Akita's fur look soft. Let's test it out in a small section to see how it looks.

Step 3: Fill in Areas With Shading

Establish which areas you want to be darker on your animal. Here, we've decided to make the top parts of our dog darker, and leave their underside a fluffy white. So, let's introduce more hatching to the other areas we want dark.

Remember to leave some areas paper-white to have highlights, even in your dark spots. It'll make your animals look just a bit more realistic!

Step 4: ADD texture to other Parts

Even though we decided to leave our dog's belly white, we can still go into that area to add some texture. Let's use small marks, and not press very hard. That will make sure the white part of its fur is still light, but add a little bit of dimension to the drawing.

Step 5: Darken your Darks

We've got our lights and our midtones in place. To decide where to put our darkest darks, imagine that a light is shining on our dog and picture in your mind where the shadows would be.

Now, let's take our pencil and add some spots of darker darks to add shadows. We'll gently add tiny bits of shadow to the white areas of fur, layering it in some spots that already have midtones. Careful not to overdo it. Then, we'll bring shadows into the other areas. Darken around the edges, and bring your darkest darks into the areas that have fur shading, leaving those paper-white spots we started with.

Step 6: Last Details

Anything missing still? On our Akita, it looks like we still need to shade its nose and tongue!

Let's do that with small, gentle strokes, keeping carefully inside the area we want to shade. Now, our good dog looks like a finished drawing!

Try it yourself! You can find the **Akita** on **Pages 74-77**.

Tips & Reminders

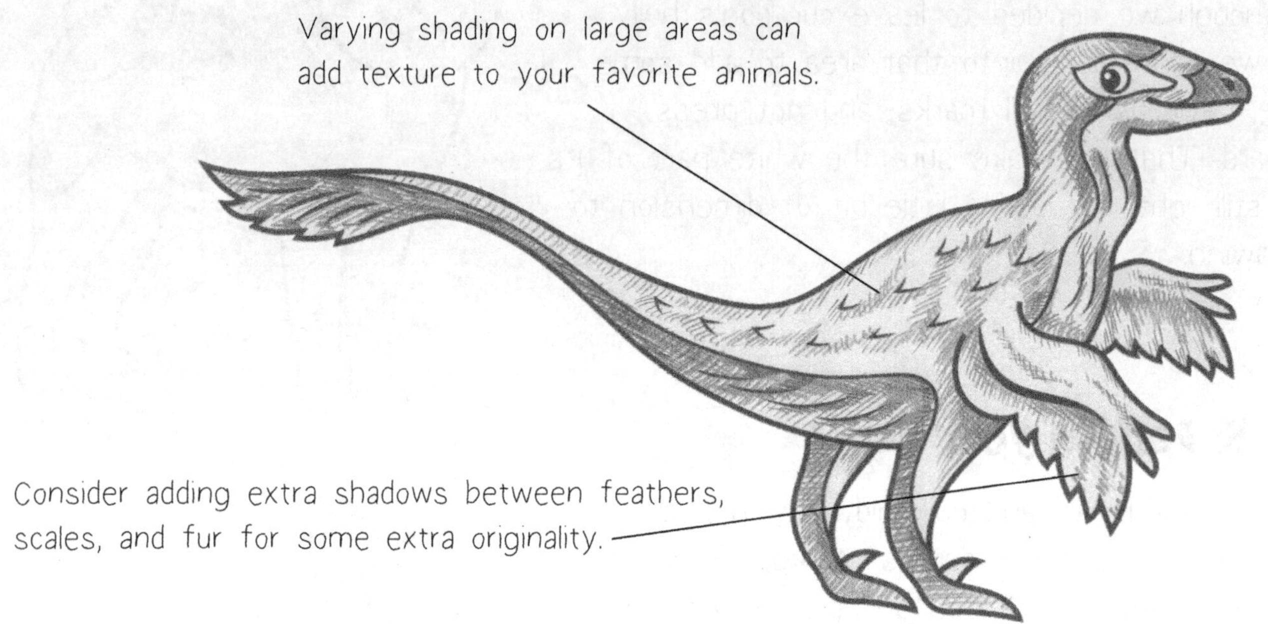

Try it yourself!
You can find the **Deinonychus** in **The Drawing Book for Kids: Dinosaurs.**

You can ink your lines and erase the pencil marks beneath before shading.

Leave the paper blank, or use an eraser for highlights.

Darkening near exterior lines makes your animal look 3D.

Try it yourself!
You can find the **Oscar fish** in **The Drawing Book for Kids: Fish.**

Most importantly: Have fun!

Dogs

Beagle

Instructions | Trace

1

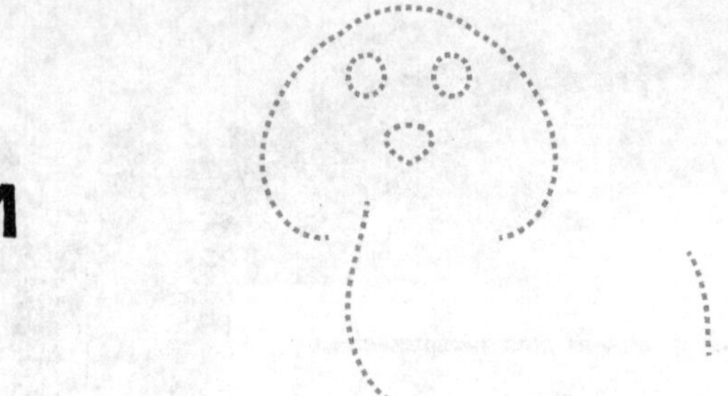

2

3

Beagle

Instructions

Trace

4

5

6

Beagle

Instructions

On Your Own

1

2

3

Beagle

Instructions | On Your Own

4

5

6

Pug

Instructions | Trace

1

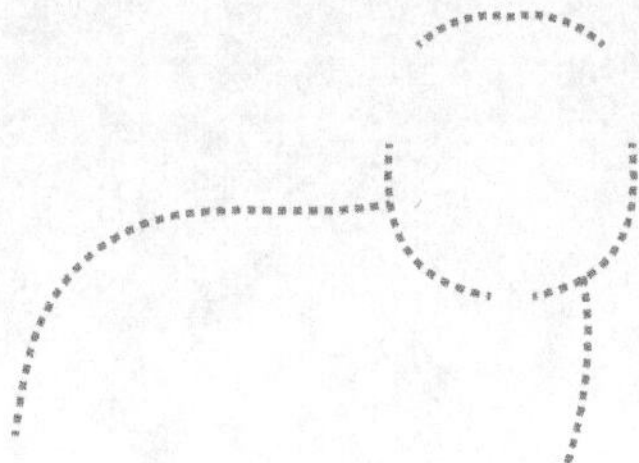

2

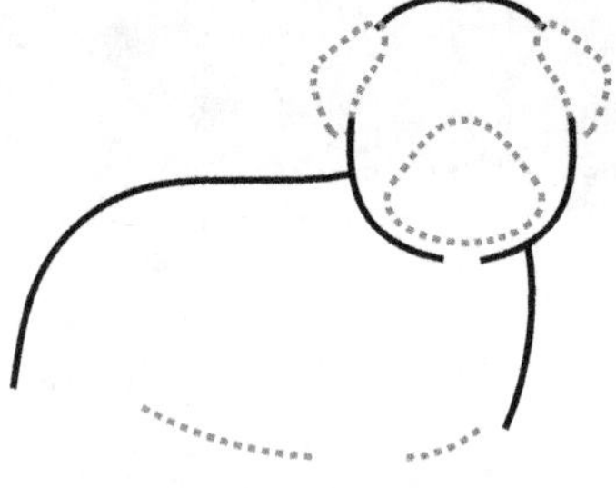

3

Pug

Instructions

Trace

4

5

6

Pug

Instructions | On Your Own

1

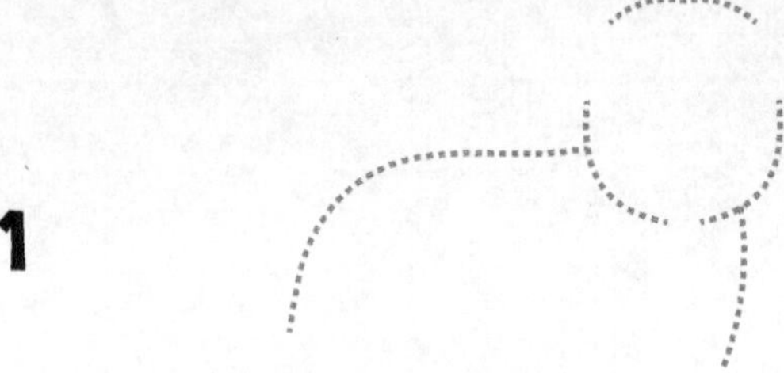

2

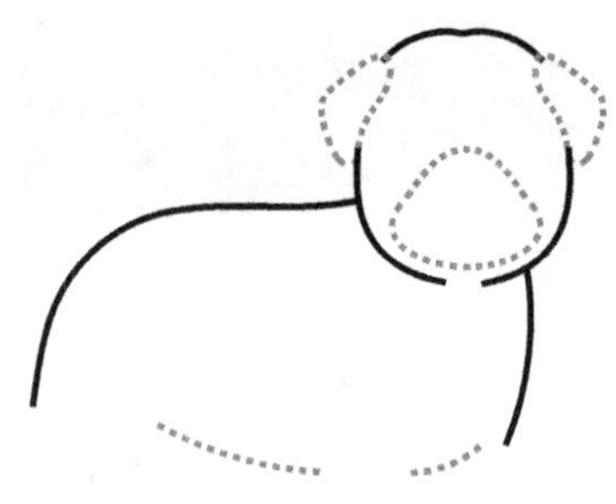

3

Pug

Instructions

On Your Own

4 

5 

6 

Chihuhua

Instructions

Trace

1

2

3

Chihuhua

Instructions

4

5

6

Chihuhua

Instructions

On Your Own

1

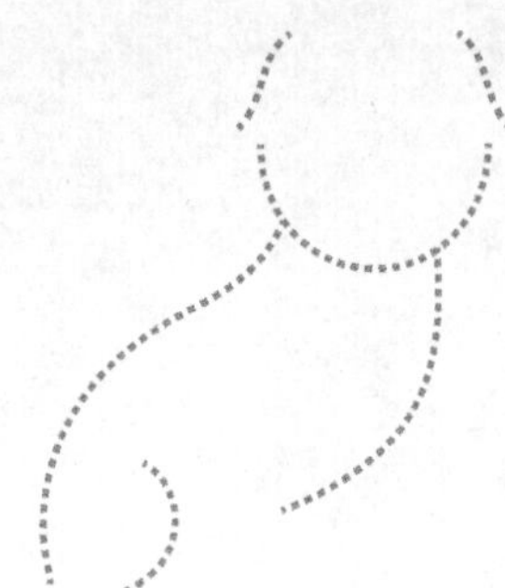

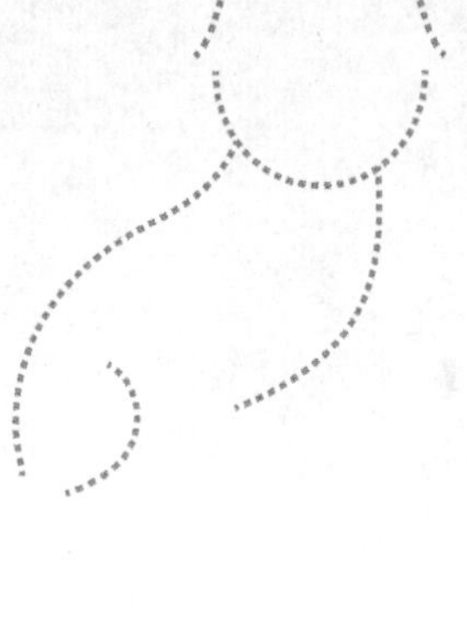

2

3

Chihuhua

Instructions

On Your Own

4

5

6

German Shepherd

Instructions

Trace

1

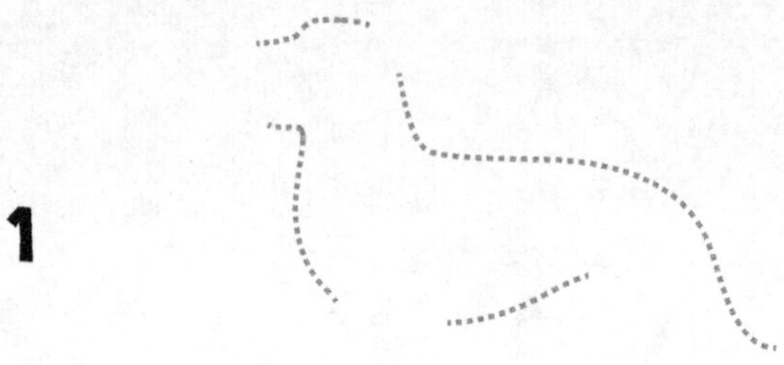

2

3

German Shepherd

Instructions

Trace

4

5

6

German Shepherd

Instructions

On Your Own

1

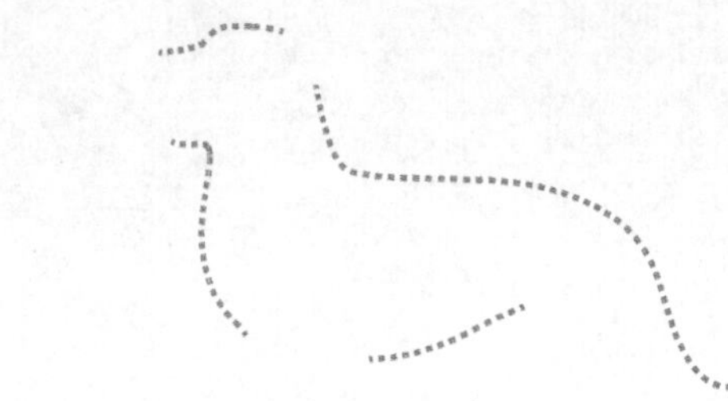

2

3

German Shepherd

Instructions

On Your Own

4

5

6

Corgi

Instructions

Trace

1

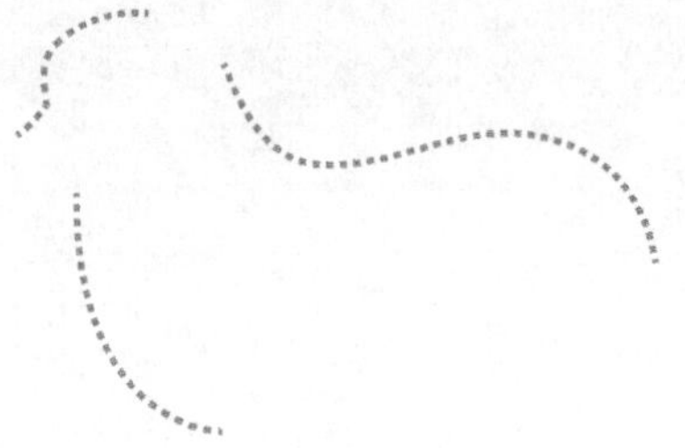

2

3

Corgi

Instructions | Trace

4

5

6

Corgi

Instructions

On Your Own

1

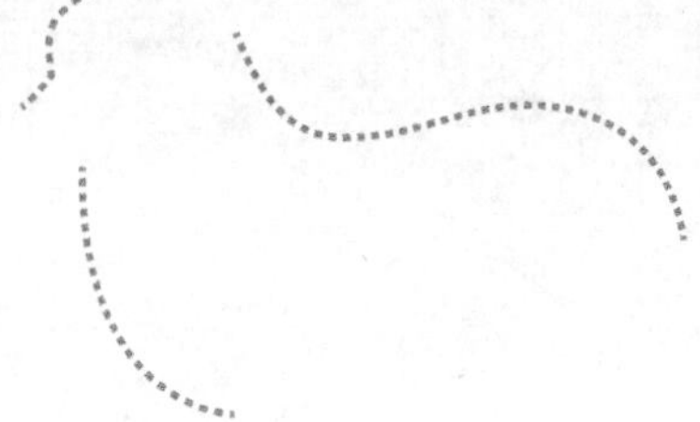

2

3

Corgi

Instructions

On Your Own

4

5

6

Basset Hound

Instructions | Trace

1

2

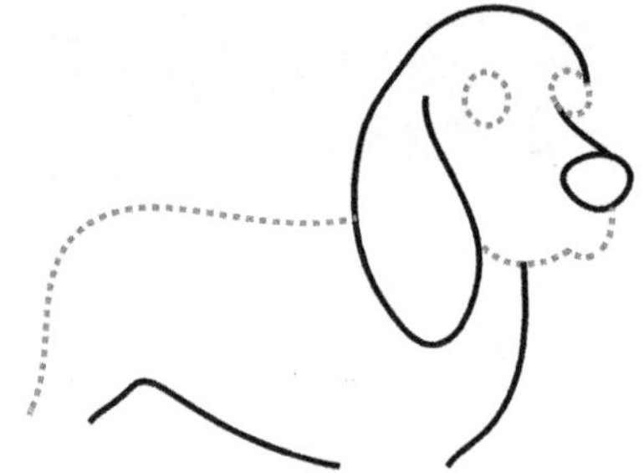

3

Basset Hound

Instructions

Trace

4

5

6

Basset Hound

Instructions

On Your Own

1

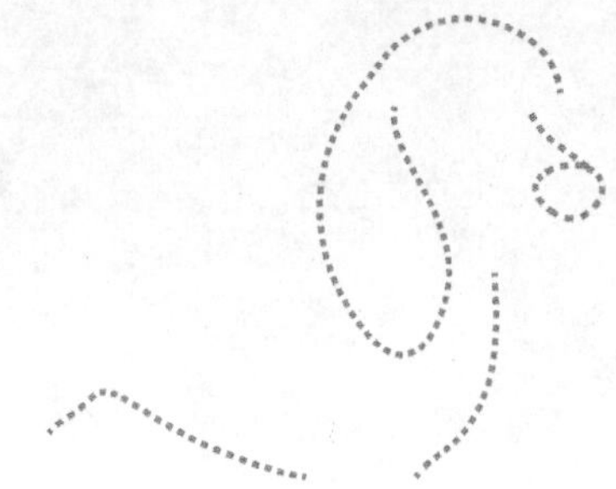

2

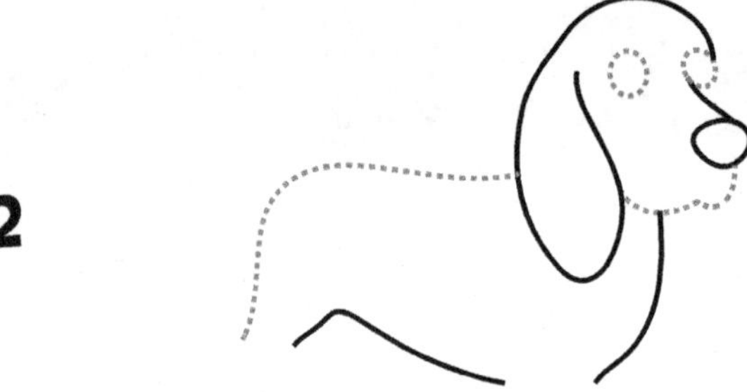

3

Basset Hound

Instructions

On Your Own

4 

5 

6 

Irish Setter

Instructions | Trace

1

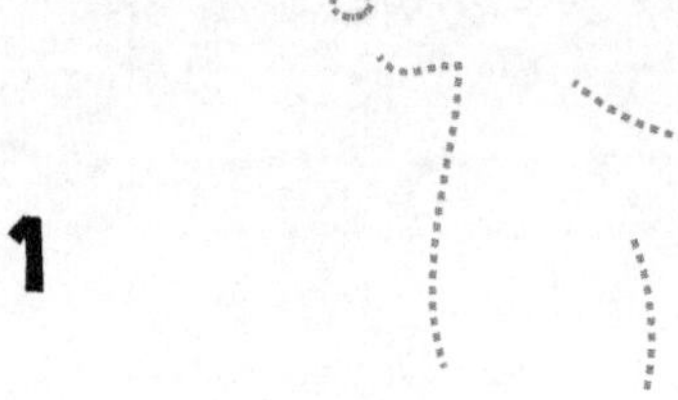

2

3

Irish Setter

Instructions

4

5

6

Irish Setter

Instructions

On Your Own

1

2

3

Irish Setter

Instructions

On Your Own

4

5

6

COONHOUND

Instructions | Trace

1

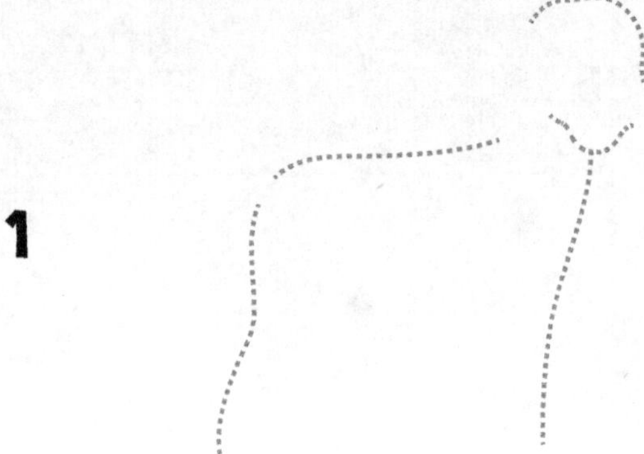

2

3

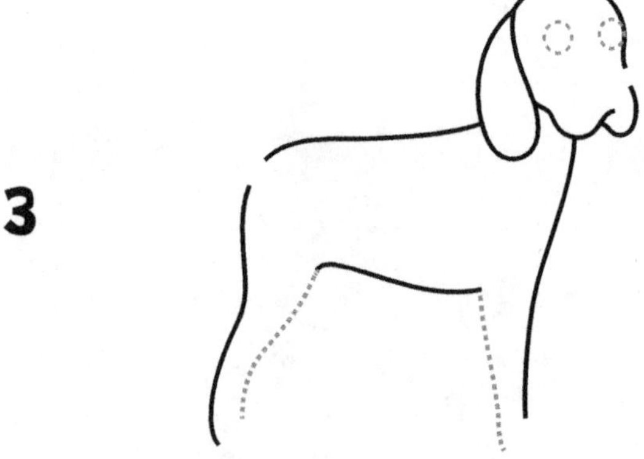

Coonhound

Instructions

Trace

4

5

6

COONHOUND

Instructions

On Your Own

1

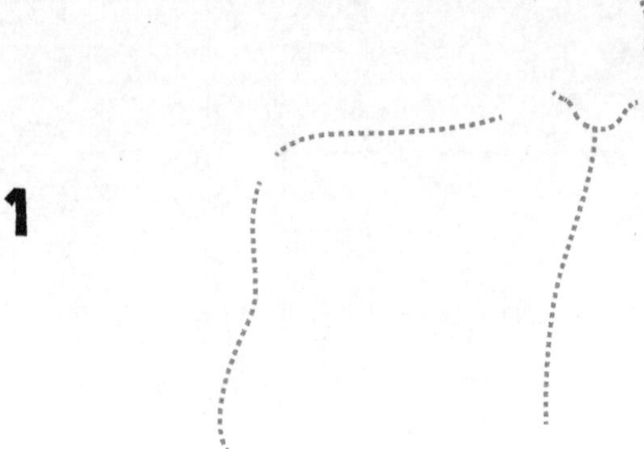

2

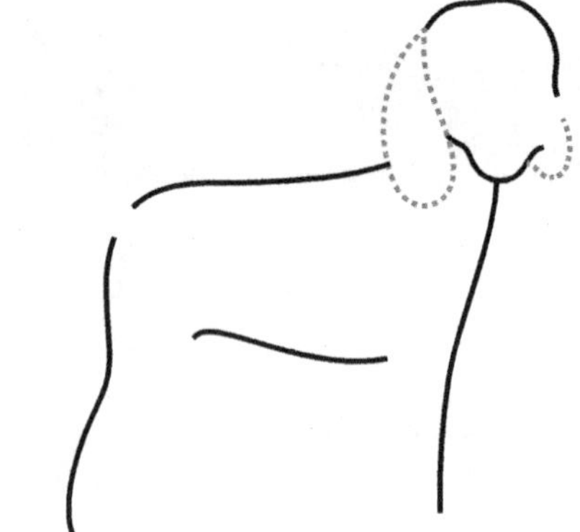

3

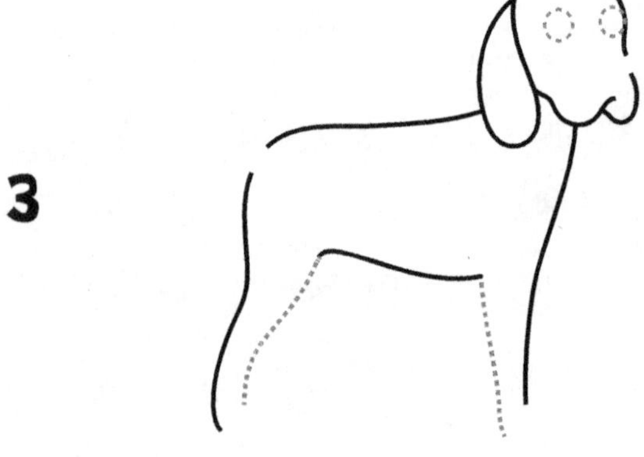

Coonhound

Instructions

On Your Own

4

5

6

Husky

Instructions

Trace

1

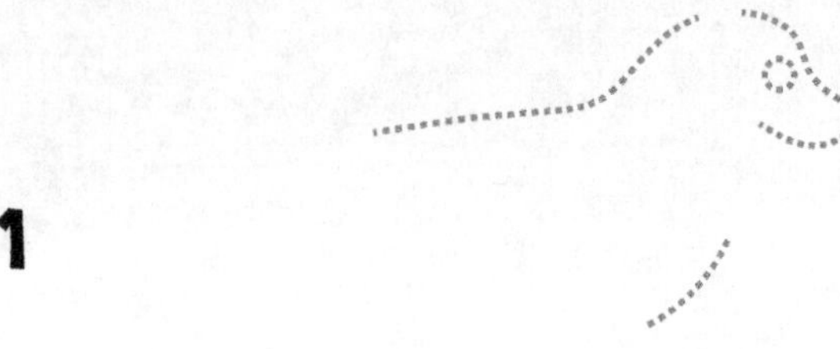

2

3

HUSKY

Instructions

Trace

4

5

6

HUSKY

Instructions | On Your Own

1

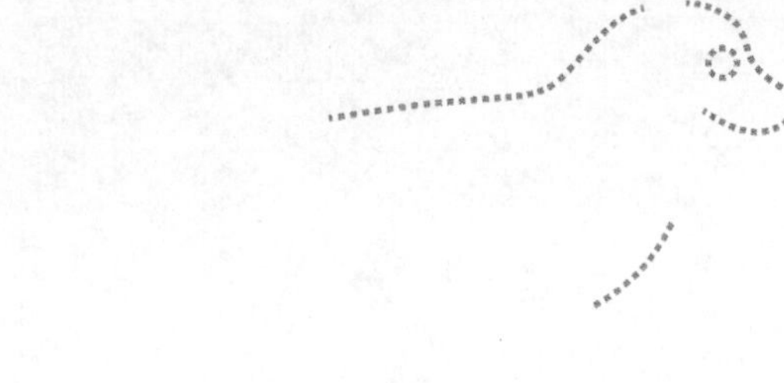

2

3

HUSKY

Instructions

On Your Own

4 

5 

6 

Whippet

Instructions

Trace

1

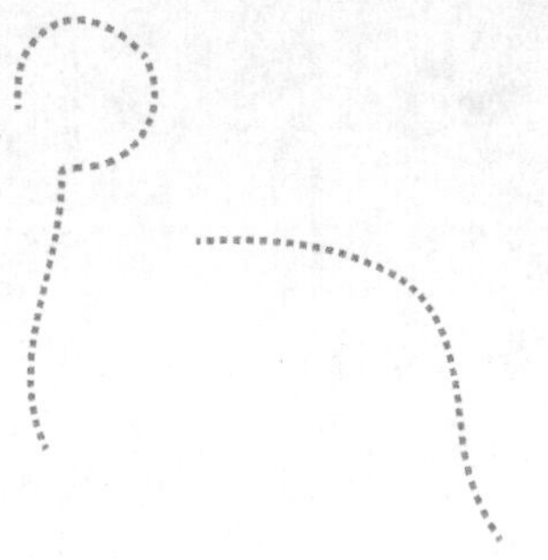

2

3

Whippet

Instructions

4

5

6

Whippet

Instructions

On Your Own

1

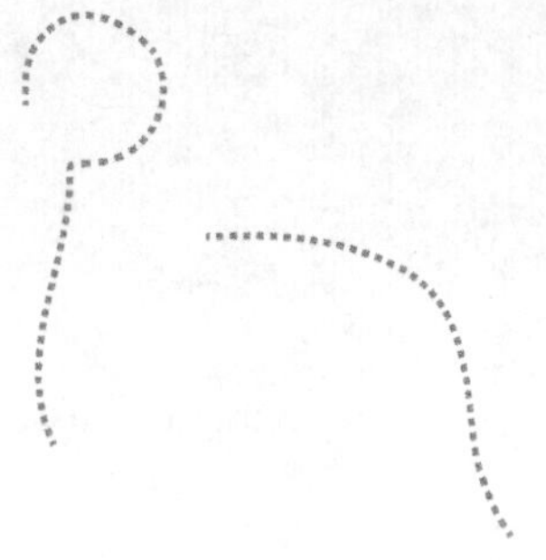

2

3

Whippet

Instructions

On Your Own

4

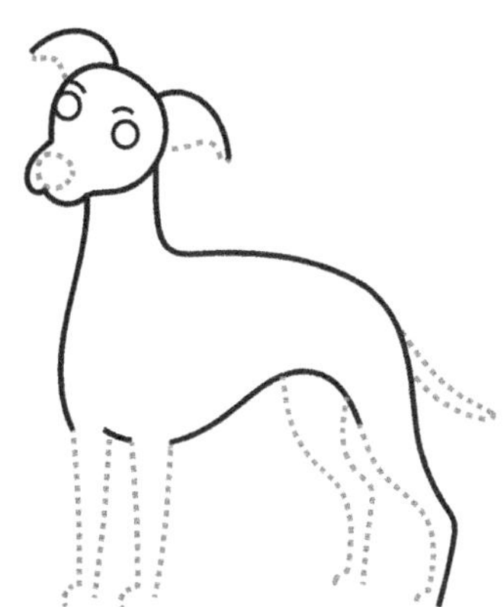

5

6

Bernese Mountain Dog

Instructions

Trace

1

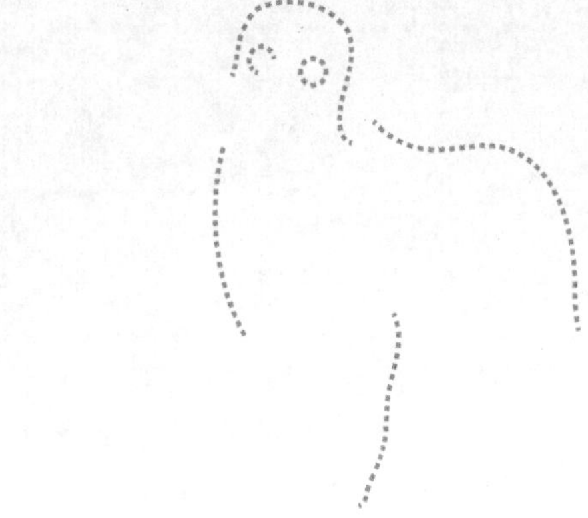

2

3

Bernese Mountain Dog

Instructions

4

5

6

Bernese Mountain Dog

Instructions

On Your Own

1

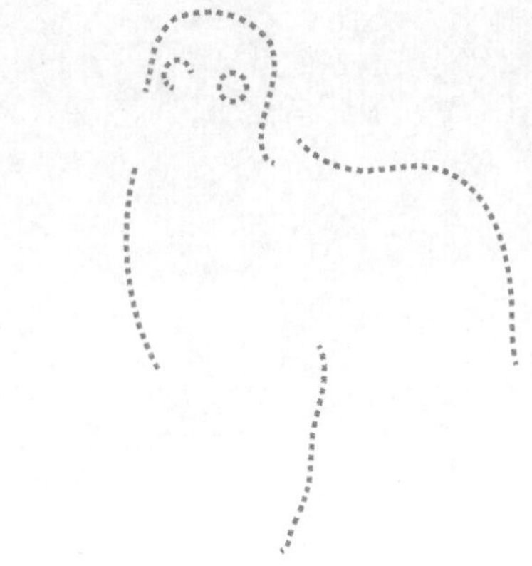

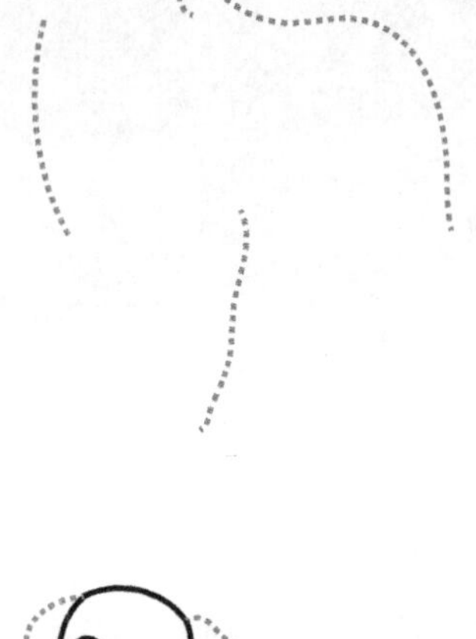

2

3

Bernese Mountain Dog

Instructions

On Your Own

4

5

6

Great Dane

Instructions

Trace

1

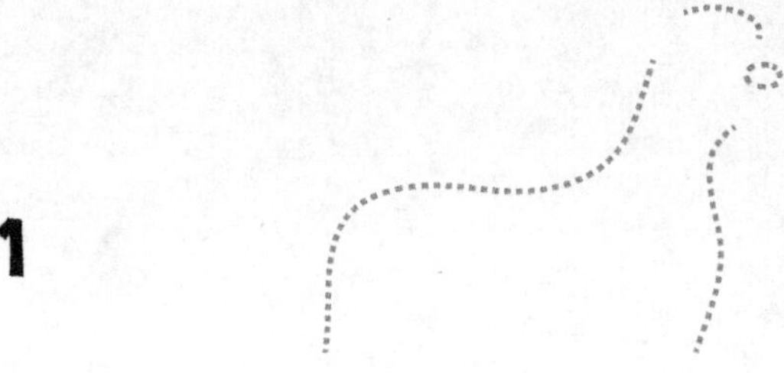

2

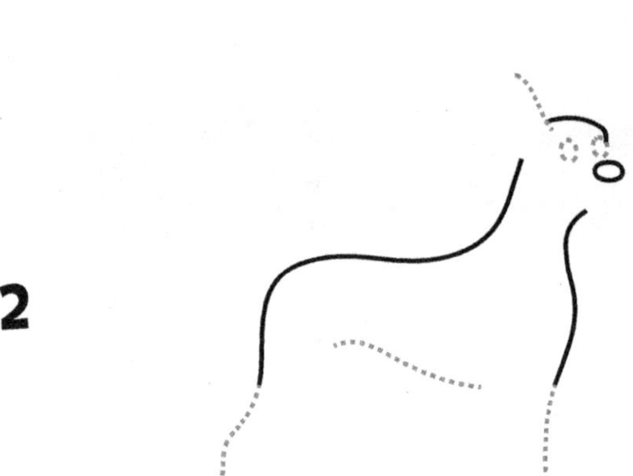

3

Great Dane

Instructions Trace

4

5

6

Great Dane

Instructions

On Your Own

1

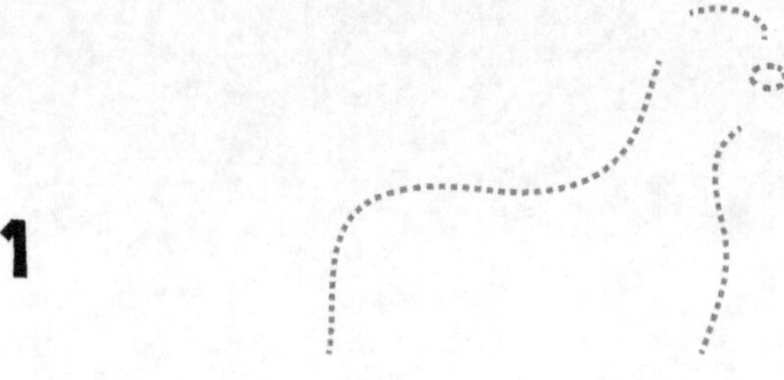

2

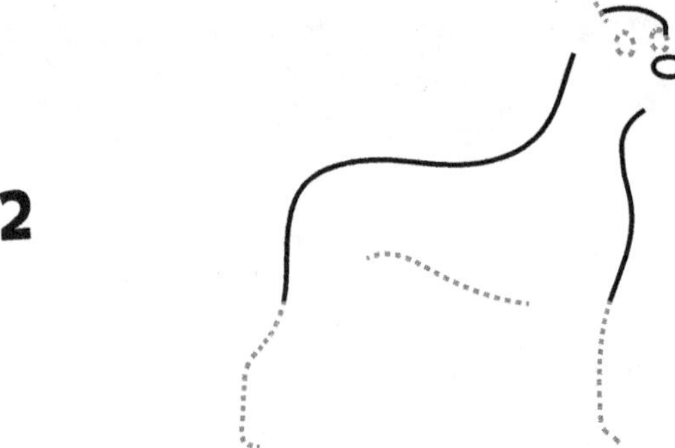

3

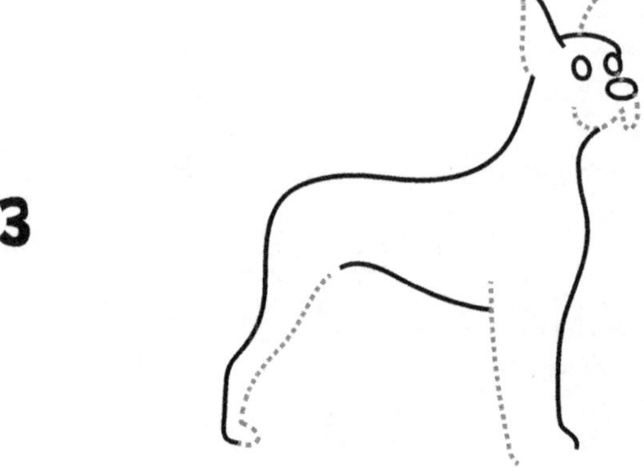

Great Dane

Instructions

On Your Own

4

5

6

Golden Retriever

Instructions | Trace

1

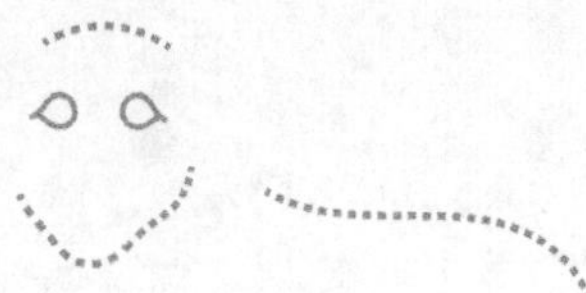

2

3

Golden Retriever

Instructions

Trace

4

5

6

GolDen Retriever

Instructions

On Your Own

1

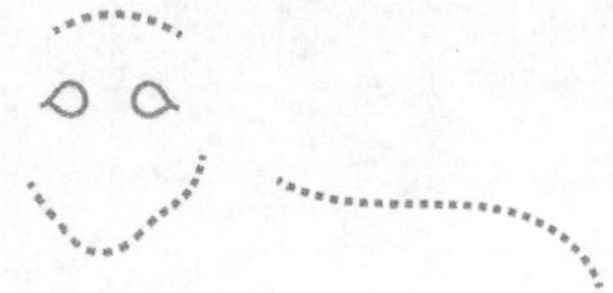

2

3

Golden Retriever

Instructions

On Your Own

4

5

6

Labrador Retriever

Instructions | Trace

1

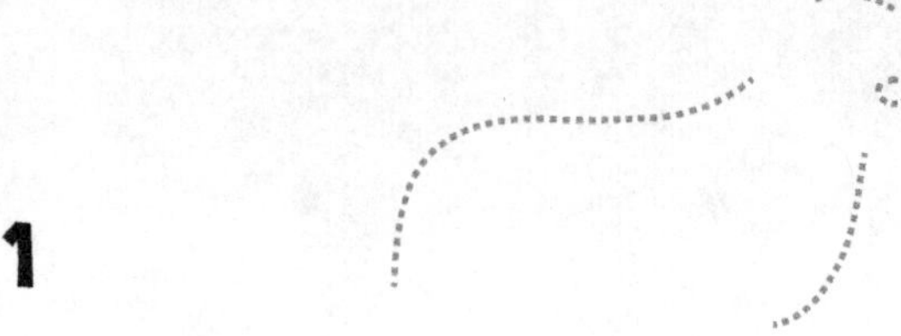

2

3

Labrador Retriever

Instructions

Trace

4

5

6

Labrador Retriever

Instructions | On Your Own

1

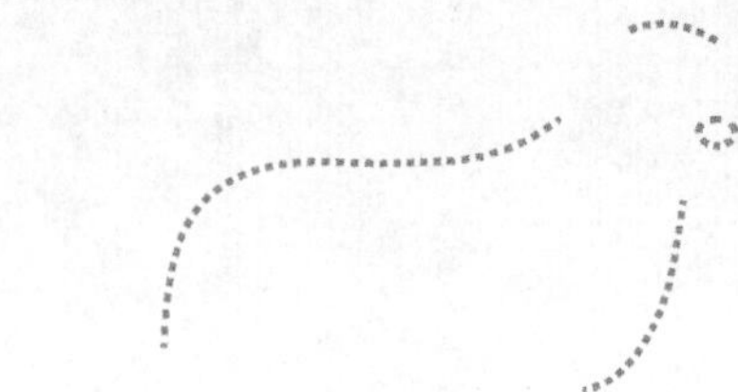

2

3

Labrador Retriever

Instructions

On Your Own

4

5

6

Boxer

	Instructions	Trace
1	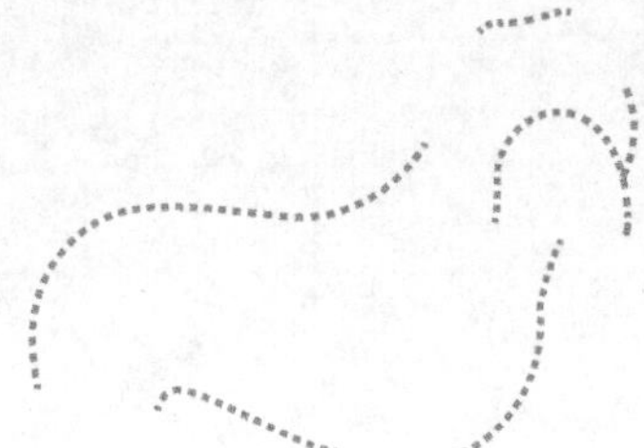	
2	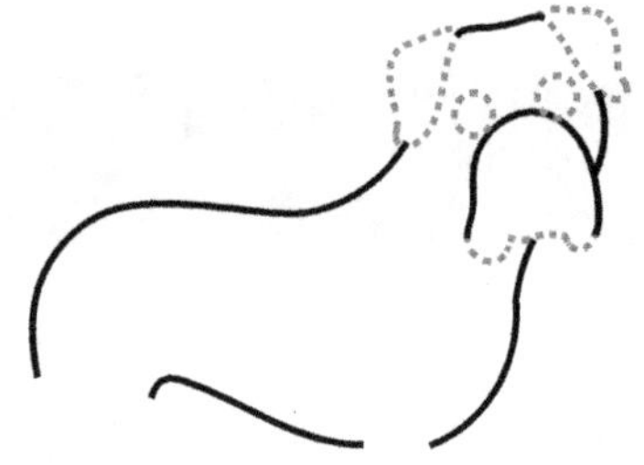	
3		

Boxer

Instructions	Trace

4  

5  

6  

Boxer

Instructions

On Your Own

1

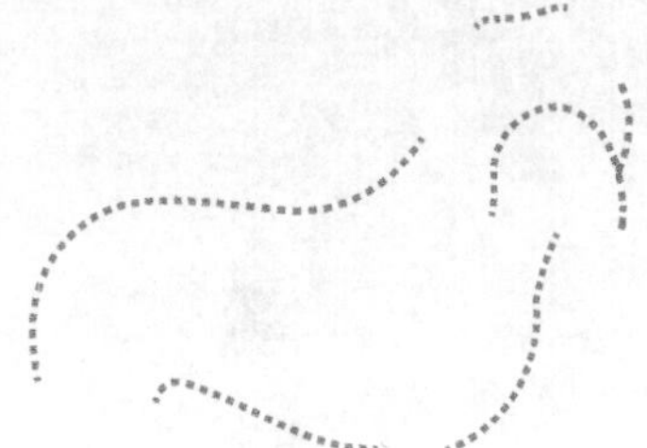

2

3

Boxer

Instructions

On Your Own

4

5

6

Pomeranian

Instructions

Trace

1

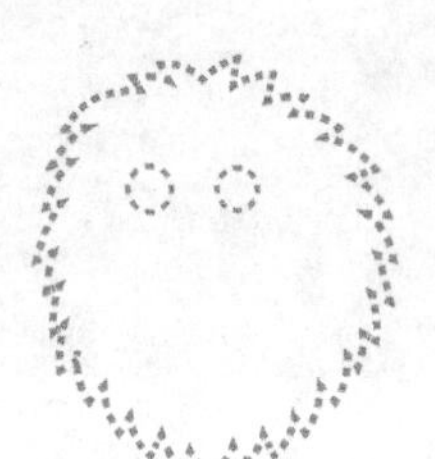

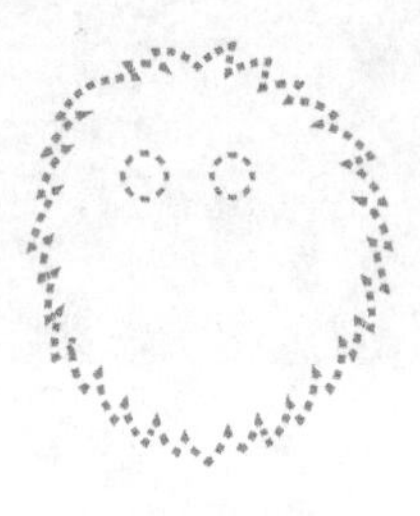

2

3

Pomeranian

Instructions

Trace

4

5

6

Pomeranian

Instructions

On Your Own

1

2

3

Pomeranian

Instructions

On Your Own

4

5

6

Dobermann

Instructions | Trace

1

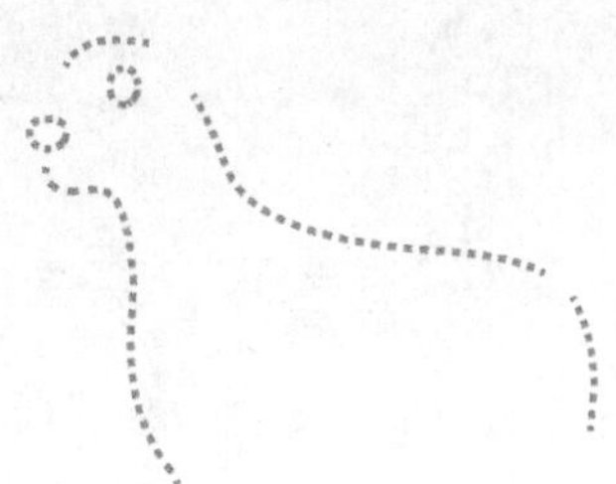

2

3

Dobermann

Instructions

4

5

6

Dobermann

Instructions | On Your Own

1

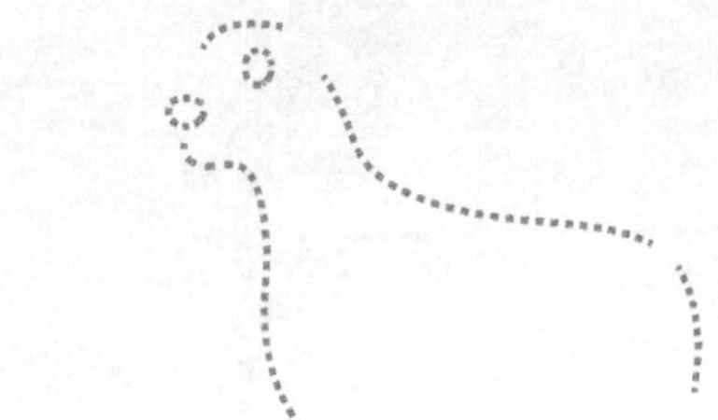

2

3

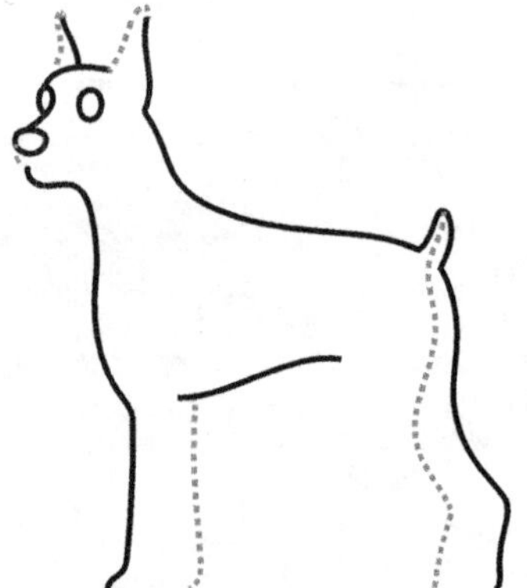

Dobermann

Instructions

On Your Own

4

5

6

Bulldog

Instructions | Trace

1

2

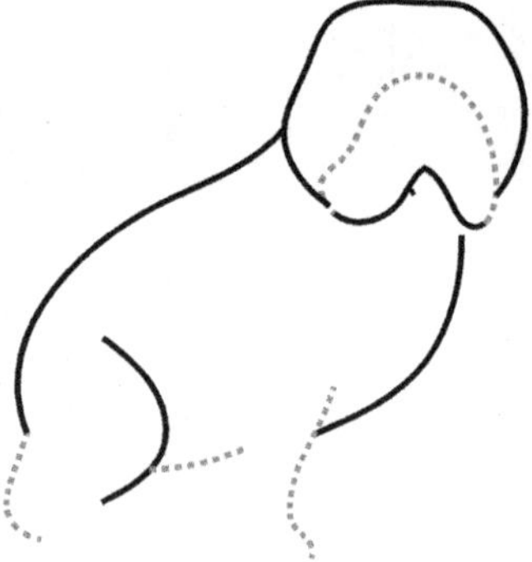

3

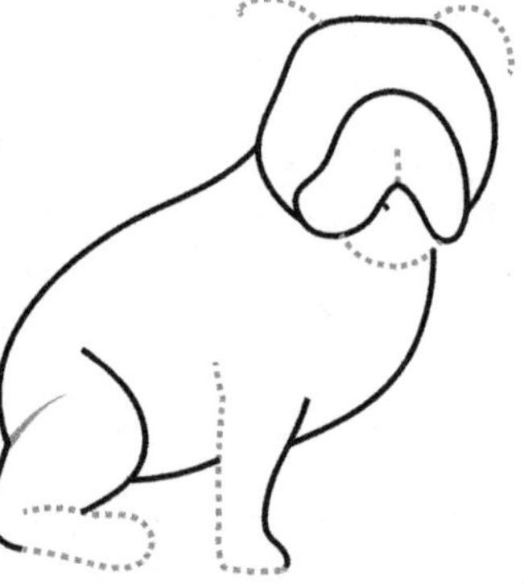

BullDog

Instructions

4  

5  

6  

BullDog

Instructions | On Your Own

1

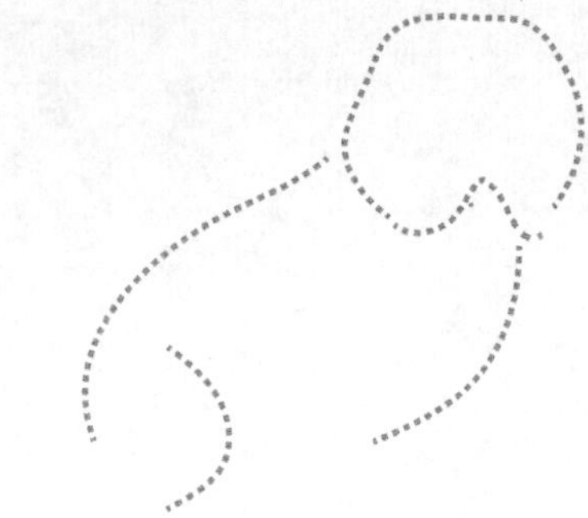

2

3

Bulldog

Instructions

On Your Own

4

5

6

Akita

Instructions

Trace

1

2

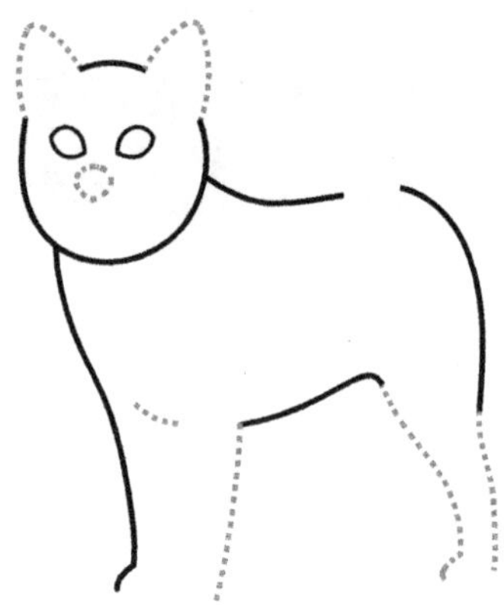

3

Akita

Instructions

4

5

6

Akita

Instructions | On Your Own

1

2

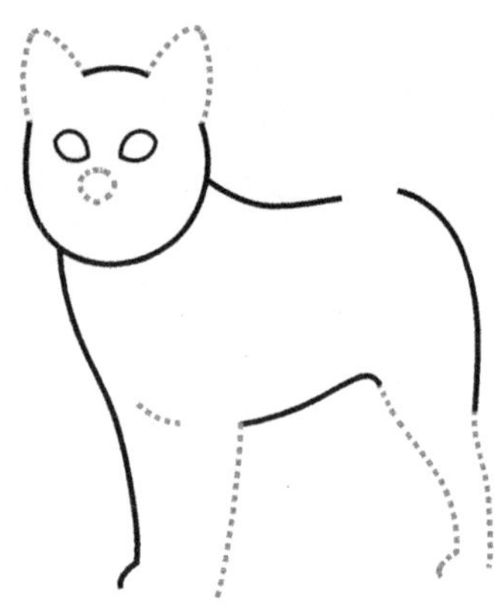

3

Akita

Instructions | On Your Own

4

5

6

French Bulldog

Instructions

Trace

1

2

3

French BullDog

Instructions

Trace

4

5

6

French BullDog

Instructions

On Your Own

1

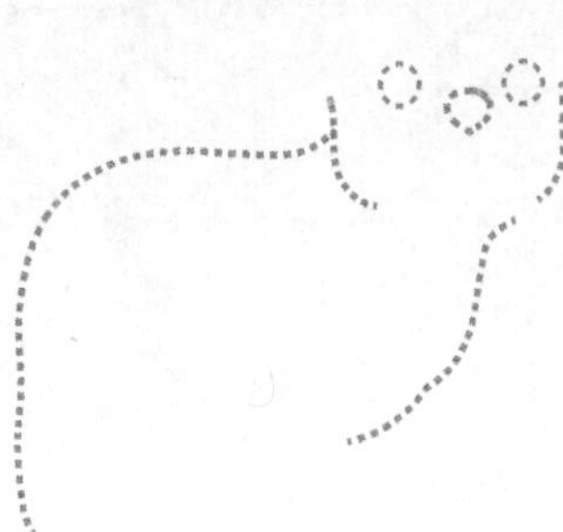

2

3

French BullDog

Instructions

On Your Own

4

5

6

PitBull

Instructions | Trace

1

2

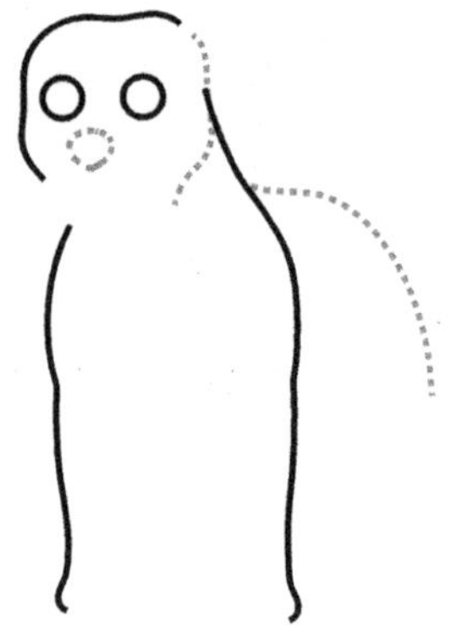

3

PitBull

Instructions

4

5

6

PitBull

Instructions

On Your Own

1

2

3

PitBull

Instructions

On Your Own

4

5

6

Beagle Puppy

Instructions

Trace

1

2

3

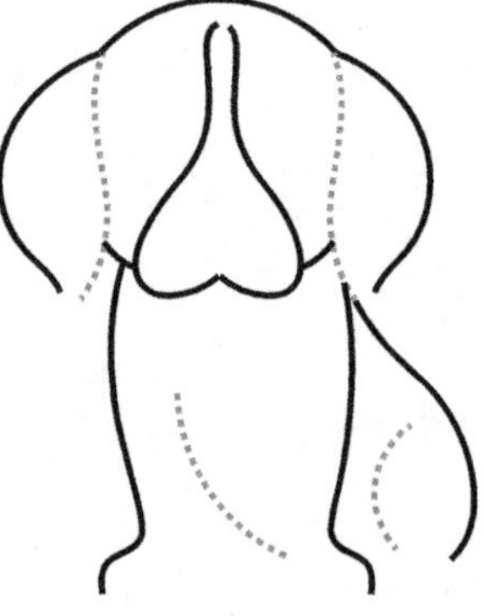

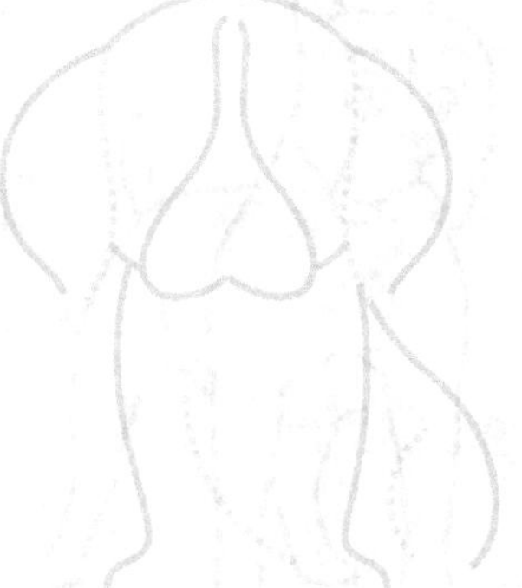

Beagle Puppy

Instructions

4

5

6

Beagle Puppy

Instructions

On Your Own

1

2

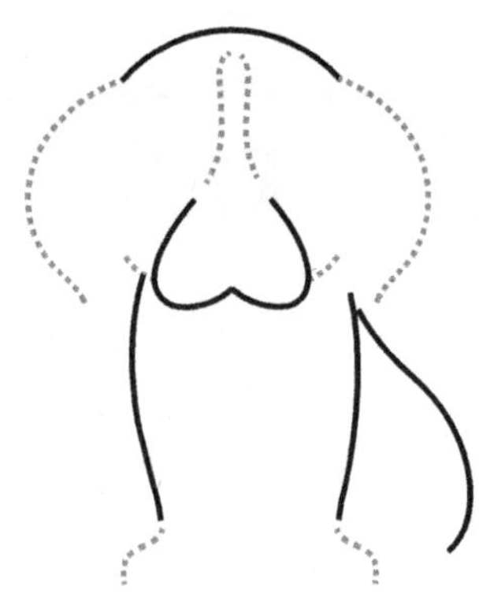

3

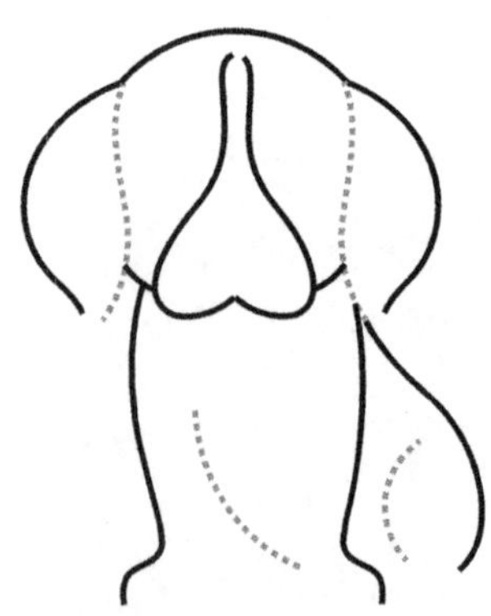

Beagle Puppy

Instructions

On Your Own

4

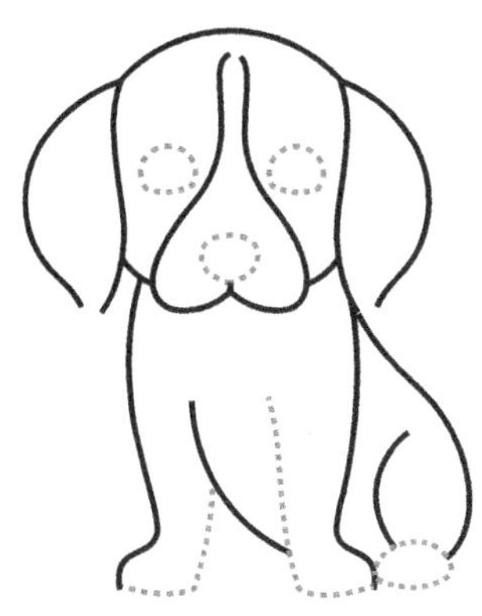

5

6

Pug Puppy

Instructions | Trace

1

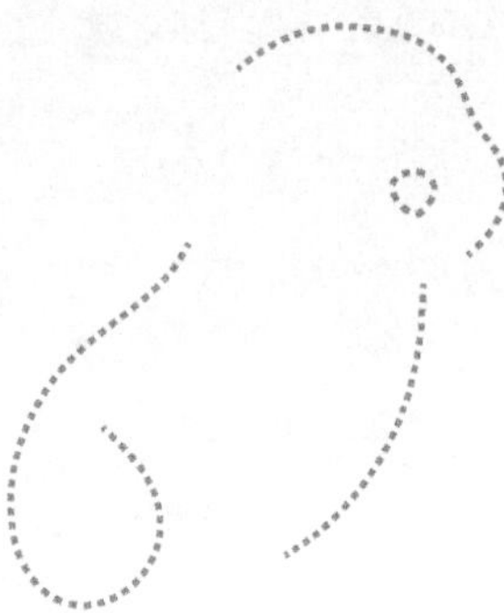

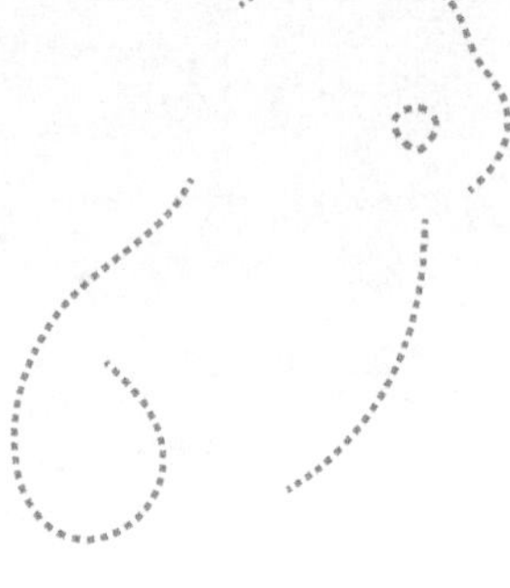

2

3

Pug Puppy

Instructions

Trace

4

5

6

Pug Puppy

Instructions | On Your Own

1

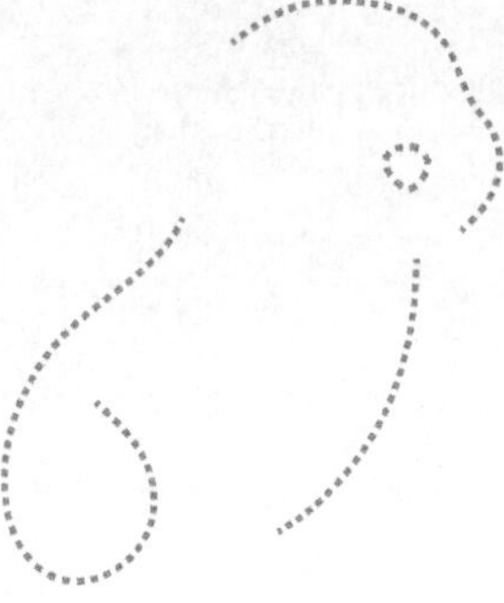

2

3

Pug Puppy

Instructions | On Your Own

4

5

6

German Shepherd Puppy

Instructions

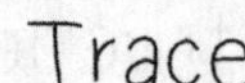
Trace

1

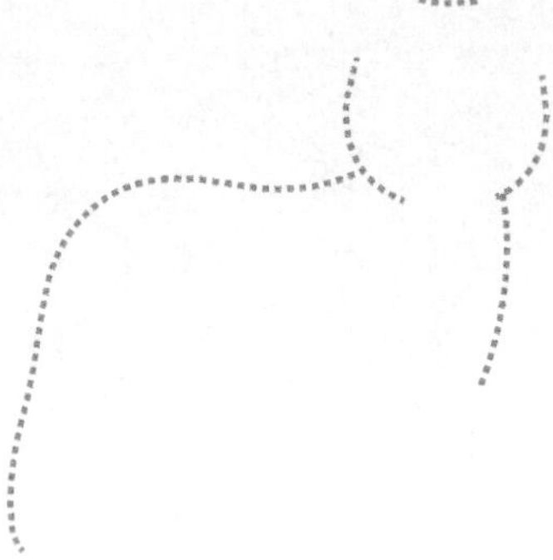

2

3

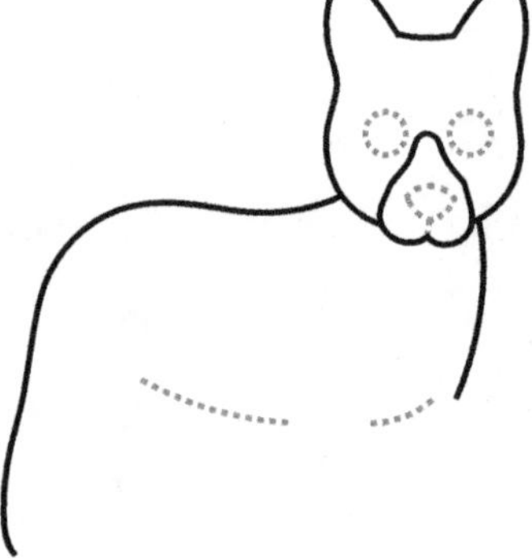

German Shepherd Puppy

Instructions   Trace

4

5

6

German Shepherd Puppy

Instructions

On Your Own

1

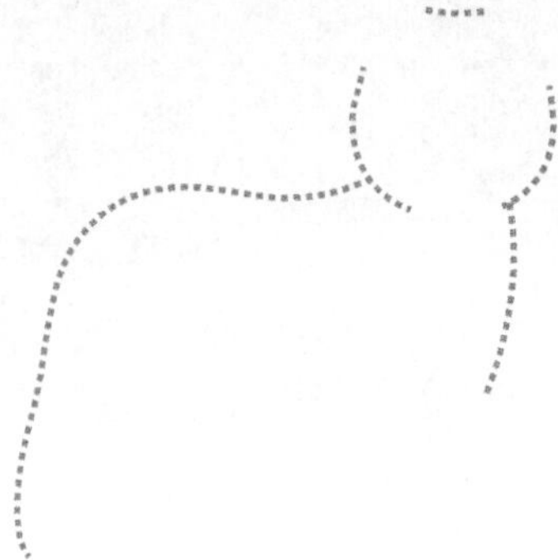

2

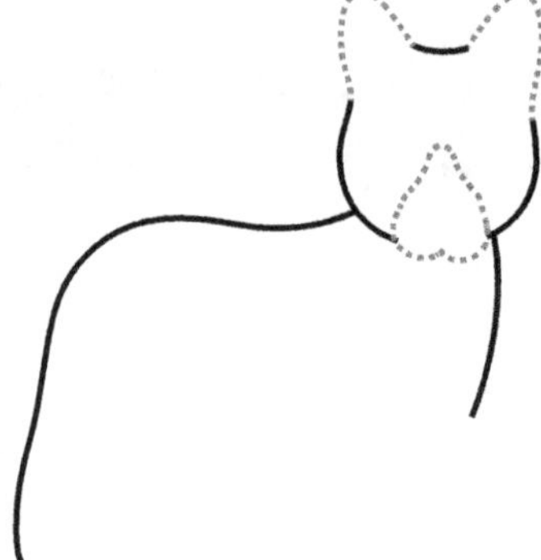

3

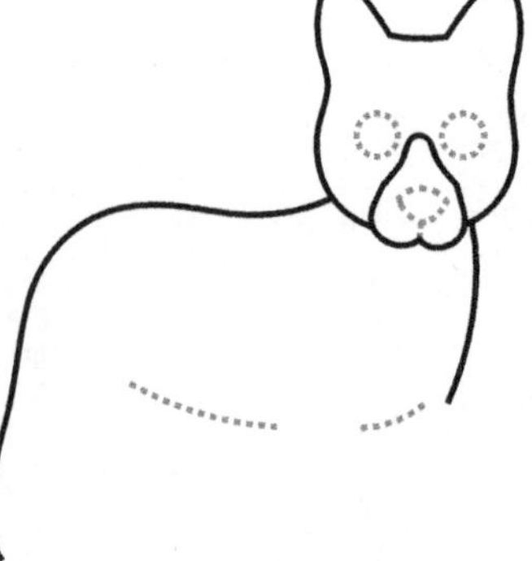

German Shepherd Puppy

Instructions

On Your Own

4

5

6

Corgi Puppy

Instructions

Trace

1

2

3

Corgi Puppy

Instructions

4

5

6

Corgi PUPPY

Instructions

On Your Own

1

2

3

Corgi Puppy

Instructions

On Your Own

4 

5 

6 

Golden Retriever Puppy

Instructions

Trace

1

2

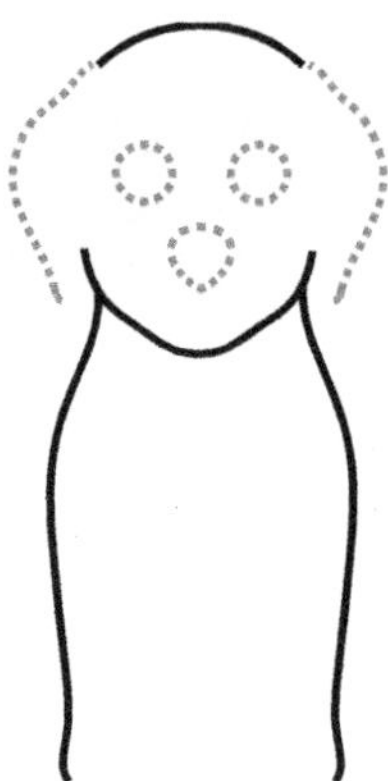

3

Golden Retriever Puppy

Instructions

4

5

6

Golden Retriever Puppy

Instructions | On Your Own

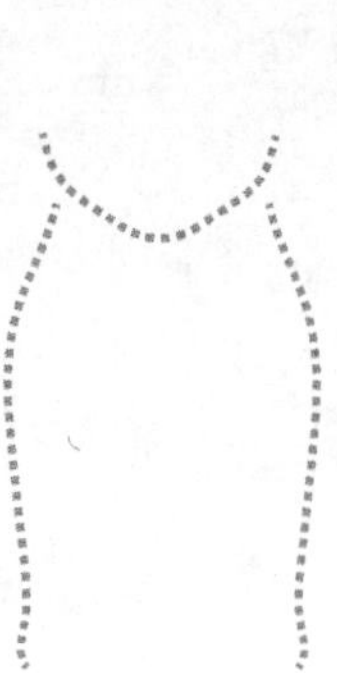

2

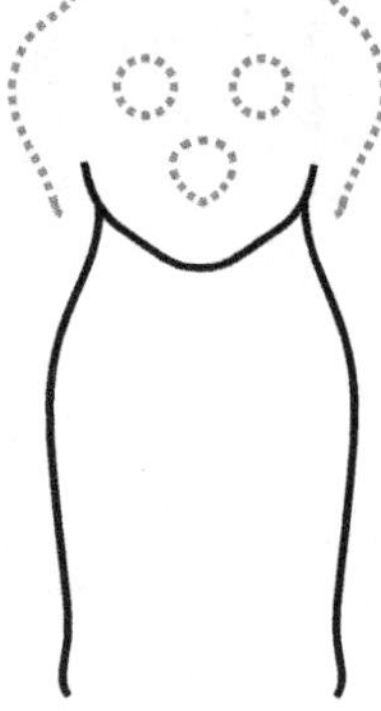

Golden Retriever Puppy

Instructions

On Your Own

4 

5 

6 

Chihuahua Puppy

Instructions

Trace

1

2

3

Chihuahua Puppy

Instructions | Trace

4

5

6

Chihuahua Puppy

Instructions

On Your Own

1

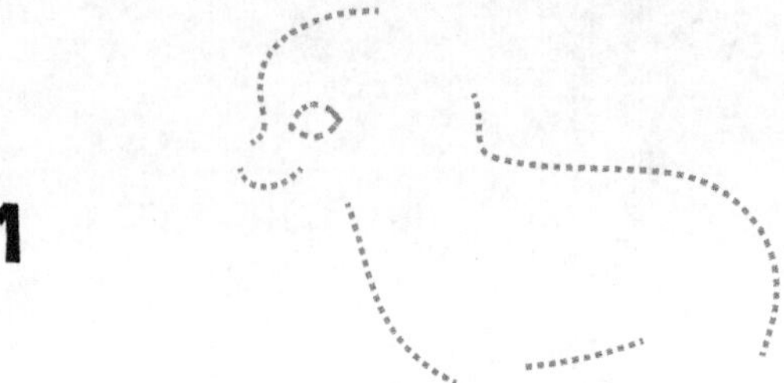

2

3

Chihuahua Puppy

Instructions

On Your Own

4

5

6

Need more space to practice?

Give it a shot here!

Made in the USA
Las Vegas, NV
03 January 2025